Loved as Promised

J. Ladd Johnson

Copyright © 2015 J. Ladd Johnson.

All rights reserved. No part of this book may be reproduced, stored, or transmitted by any means—whether auditory, graphic, mechanical, or electronic—without written permission of both publisher and author, except in the case of brief excerpts used in critical articles and reviews. Unauthorized reproduction of any part of this work is illegal and is punishable by law.

Scripture verses marked KJV are from the King James Version of the Bible.

Scripture quotations marked "NKJV" are taken from the New King James Version. Copyright © 1982 by Thomas Nelson, Inc. Used by permission. All rights reserved.

ISBN: 978-0-5781-6347-5 (sc)
ISBN: 978-0-5781-6348-2 (hc)
ISBN: 978-0-5781-6346-8 (e)

Library of Congress Control Number: 2015908445

Because of the dynamic nature of the Internet, any web addresses or links contained in this book may have changed since publication and may no longer be valid. The views expressed in this work are solely those of the author and do not necessarily reflect the views of the publisher, and the publisher hereby disclaims any responsibility for them.

Any people depicted in stock imagery provided by Thinkstock are models, and such images are being used for illustrative purposes only.
Certain stock imagery © Thinkstock.

Lulu Publishing Services rev. date: 6/22/2015

CONTENTS

Preface ix
Acknowledgments xi
Introduction xiii

Chapter 1   Love: The "Fairy-Tale" Version 1
Chapter 2   Love in the Wilderness 11
Chapter 3   Forgive and Let Go 21
Chapter 4   Fellowship and Friends 31
Chapter 5   Restoration 39
Chapter 6   Waiting 47
Chapter 7   The Arrival 57
Chapter 8   The Courtship 67
Chapter 9   The Proposal 75
Chapter 10   The Wedding 79

Epilogue 89

DEDICATION

This book is dedicated to my husband, Lee, who encouraged me to write my story as an assignment given by God. You possess all the qualities that any woman would want in a mate. Thank you for your prayers and for your emotional and spiritual support as I navigated through the challenges of sharing aspects of my life that I pray will make a difference in the lives of many women.

PREFACE

Writing *Love as Promised* was truly an assignment given by God, one chapter at a time. There were times when I wanted to abort the assignment, but God would not allow me to do it. I lay awake many sleepless nights, thinking of the assignment with a sense of urgency and restlessness.

God also placed key people in my path who expressed a need for the work I had begun even though they had no knowledge of my writings. Many women talked to me about their struggles with their relationships and were seeking answers. I had been there and understood their sense of confusion and their need to find direction in their lives. They found inspiration in my love story and encouraged me to write a book, but it was not enough. God's hand was more convincing, and I knew I had to do the assignment to plant the seed of hope He had given me. In return, I also knew that He would water this seed and take care of the assignment. My assignment is to give you the hope of finding love and happiness the way God intended.

 ACKNOWLEDGMENTS

I'd like to thank my beloved daughters, Tenisha, Jameelah, and Rasheedah, who encouraged me to write my first poem when writing was not yet part of my repertoire. I told them I was not a writer, but they responded by saying, "Mom, everyone's a poet. You can write." It was during the process of writing that I discovered I had something to share and that I truly enjoyed the experience.

I'd also like thank my sister, Erma, for the many hours she dedicated to help me refine the work and husband, Jamar, for his encouragement and heartfelt prayers.

INTRODUCTION

My family of origin migrated to Las Vegas in the early 1950s from Fordyce, Arkansas, looking for a better way of life. I was the last of six children born in a city that attracts tourists from all over the world through its entertainment industry. People are surprised to learn that I grew up in a neighborhood with schools, churches, libraries, and beautiful parks, largely because Las Vegas has been advertised as the number one destination to indulge in gaming with its lavish hotels and casinos. Many people have said it's not a "family-oriented place." What also sets Las Vegas apart from most cities is its colorful bright lights that never fail to excite tourists, who come to town to play. Tourists very seldom venture off the beaten path of the Strip or downtown Las

Vegas to understand the real lives of the people who live and raise their families in the city's communities. Las Vegas is often referred to as Sin City, and many visitors believe that no godly thing could possibly come out of Las Vegas or thrive in this dry, deserted land that sits in a dust bowl surrounded by mountains, but I beg to differ. As a native who grew up in Las Vegas, my experience was very different. I often ask visitors to take a second look because there is more here than meets the eye. God has planted roses in the desert, a symbol of beauty, hope, and promise, which is where my story begins.

I grew up in a diverse community within Las Vegas that was heavily influenced by southern traditions, and churches and families were valued commodities. Many families had migrated from the South and settled in what became known as the Westside, also known as the "Mississippi of the West." Black and Hispanic families lived near downtown Las Vegas. Native Americans lived on the reservation, close to the railroad tracks north of downtown. Families came looking for work in construction, the casinos, and the entertainment industry and they also worked government, city, and county jobs. My dad was one of those who had secured a government job working at the Nevada Test Site, north of Las Vegas city limits.

Our community had a small-town appeal where relationships were respected and protected. Neighbors valued each other's feelings and were careful not to offend, and even today, I'm very empathetic toward others' feelings. We attended church and worshipped together, prayed together, and lived together. Many tourists would vacation in Las Vegas—most likely, some less fortunate than when they had arrived—nevertheless, the neighbors were there to stay, creating a community of support.

It was not unusual for Mom to send me next door to borrow some flour from our neighbor, who would drop in for an evening meal from time to time. Dad would fish and hunt with his buddies, many with whom he carpooled, bringing home trout and bass, rabbit, and venison to stock the freezer. Mothers and fathers watched over the neighborhood children as we rode our bikes, played hopscotch, and jumped rope while chanting "Little Sally Walker." Our parents expressed gratitude when neighbors corrected their children for misbehaving. When we returned home, we were disciplined and directed to apologize to those we had offended.

Whereas gaming and adult entertainment attracted tourists, most families were attracted to the downtown area, where we shopped for food and clothing and, in early spring, celebrated Helldorado Days.

My family would arrive for the Helldorado Days parade early on Saturday morning. We would search for the best place to sit, in our lawn chairs, and watch the decorated floats, horses, and marching bands parade by. For shade, some families sat in the city park, adjacent to the parade, under a canopy of large fruitless mulberry trees. Others families sat on blankets that covered the scorching concrete sidewalk while we enjoyed snow cones and cotton candy in our favorite flavors.

Photography was Dad's favorite hobby this time of the year. He would create a slide show of the parade, which entertained our family at home on days when it was too hot to play outside. The parade ended every year with Clydesdale horses prancing down Fremont Street on their white furry, feathered legs as the crowd cheered them on. After the parade, all of us walked to Cashman Field to attend the carnival and the rodeo; the "cowboys" were in town.

Our family made frequent visits to Lake Mead Recreation Area or the Las Vegas City Pool to keep cool in the heat of the summer. After the first snowfall at Mount Charleston, we made the annual pilgrimage to ride homemade cardboard sleds down the sides of snow-covered hills, to roast marshmallows over an open pit, and to enjoy a cup of hot chocolate to warm our bodies. The movie theaters and city parks and recreation centers were popular places for family entertainment as well.

On school nights, we were in bed by nine o'clock, but in the summer, families stayed up late into the evening as the temperatures cooled and the sky lit up with neon lights. My friends and I played games barefooted in the front yard and sank our toes into cool blades of grass. Our parents watched out for us by leaving their front doors open or by sitting on their front porches as we played. As the evening wore on, I could hear our parents calling for us to come into the house when it was time for bed.

At thirty years of age, I noticed a change in the makeup of the families in our community. There were more single mothers who were becoming the heads of their households, and many of my peers were raising children without a father in the home. Also, church congregations began to mirror this shift in family structure as more women than men became active churchgoers. I could not understand this phenomenon. What was happening to two-parent families? What was causing the shift in family structure? Had love, marriage, and family become obsolete, a rarity shared only by those fortunate enough to find it? As I pondered my thoughts, I saw despair on the faces of many women who had suffered broken relationships and been denied the blessings that come with love, marriage, and family. I wondered if this sense of despair was affected by the culture of Las Vegas. As I grew older and began to travel, I discovered that many women were experiencing the same fate across the country.

I could not write about love for many years, because I too became a casualty of love and experienced the same despair as a single parent. I lived in fear that I would go to my grave never experiencing the "once-in-a-lifetime" true love and marriage I so desired. I struggled to find my "love story," to make sense of it all, to understand why so many women were in the same predicament and shared the same sentiment. I decided to write this book, to share my love story in the most honest way I could, as a testament to God's love and grace.

Some names, in my story, have been changed to respect the privacy of family and friends.

I am one of those roses that God watered in the desert that blossomed and received love as promised, for which I am truly grateful. I could not do it alone. I fell short of God's glory on many occasions, but He extended His grace and reconciled me to Himself. I pray that this book will bring you inspiration and shine a beacon of light along your journey to find love the way God intended.

CHAPTER 1

Love: The "Fairy-Tale" Version

Train up a child in the way he should go: and when he is old, he will not depart from it.

—Proverbs 22:6 KJV

I believed as a little girl that my destiny was to love someone for a lifetime. At one o'clock in the afternoon, the neighborhood became quiet; no one was in sight as temperatures soared above 105 degrees. I would find a cool spot on the couch, under the swamp cooler, to watch classic love movies. My eyes were glued to the television. A tapestry rug depicting deer running in the woods hung on the wall above the black-and-white screen. There was something magical about love stories, which imprinted lessons that supposedly taught me what "real love" looked and felt like. My playmates were at home watching the same love stories on their televisions. Later, we would role-play scripts, which became a part of our dramatic play with dolls, play ovens, Mom's pearl necklace, earrings, and high-heeled shoes. Playing house and dress-up did not interest the boys; they wanted to ride bikes, shoot marbles, and catch lizards and tortoises. However, this did not deter the girls from practicing to become perfect mates, as marriage and family was our destiny. What I didn't realize at the age of ten was that our role models were jumping in and out of marriages with some of their costars.

As the story line went, two people would meet and fall in love at first sight, or the man would be smitten by the woman, who would initially resist his advances. Craftily, he would pursue and win her love in the end because his life would be unbearable without her.

The lovable ones were portrayed as beautiful and desirable, discovered at one glance, deserving that ultimate act, the marriage proposal: when the man bowed down on one knee with a diamond ring and said, "Will you marry me?" The woman would look totally surprised, teary eyed, as if she hadn't seen it coming, accepting his proposal with gratitude. Plain Jane didn't succeed at winning the affection of her man; clever she may have been, but she wasn't pretty enough, losing out to someone with a better package than hers. Neither did the scarlet woman, who had seen better days, have any success. Her air of desperation and tattered appearance drove her man into the arms of another woman more beautiful by comparison. I often wondered, outside of their looks, what did these beautiful women possessed that captured the hearts of their leading stars. What was the attraction, the special ingredient? Interestingly, I rarely got a glimpse of what their love was like after the "I do" part, but it didn't stop me from fantasizing about love. I came to believe that it was the woman's physical beauty, the perfect configuration of her face, body, and hair, with an innocence that almost appeared as naiveté, dressed in fashionable couture, that won her the man of her dreams.

I pondered these thoughts as puberty made its early claim on me, transforming the body of a twelve-year-old into a physically mature woman. How shy and embarrassed I felt as young boys, who were unpredictable and silly, tried their hands at dating me but lacked the finesse to woo a young lady. As I grew older, my fascination turned toward older men who were more mature and seasoned. They appeared suave and better able to deliver the love package that would guarantee a happily-ever-after life.

My parents' love appeared boring; it lacked the passion that I had seen on television. Displays of affection were not common for them at home. When I did see my parents display affection, during my younger years, I felt embarrassed at seeing them kiss as I grappled to make sense of their love. Dad was old school and, like "real" men, kept his feelings close to his chest, letting them surface only when his frustration reached a boiling point.

Nevertheless, listening to stories that Dad and Mom told led me to believe there was something special between them. Dad sometimes reminisced about how he'd met Mom on the college campus where she was studying to become a teacher (young men often went there to meet college girls). When he saw her, he was smitten by her beauty and smarts. Mom noticed that Dad stood out from other young men, with his mature, charming ways and fancy clothes, driving a Model-T Ford. And so, they began to date.

Dad worked two jobs to court Mom in style; they wined, dined, and did the jitterbug to the sounds of Duke Ellington,

Glen Miller, and Tommy Dorsey, which became known as Dad's favorite collection of music. I grew up and acquired a liking for Dad's music while my peers were busy watching Dick Clark's *American Bandstand* and, in my teen years, *Soul Train*. One of my favorite tunes by Duke Ellington was "Take the 'A' Train."

During the early years of their marriage, Mom taught Dad how to read, as he had grown up in the South with a third-grade education, attending school between planting and harvesting seasons. Most evenings, Dad would come in from work, place his cowboy boots next to his favorite recliner, and read his outdoorsman sport magazines and watched the six o'clock news. Mom would prepare the family meal, and Dad was proud of the fact that he had influenced her cooking abilities. Dad had entered the United States Navy during World War II as a cook just after the Japanese bombed Pearl Harbor. After the war, mom and dad had six children. I imagined that by the time I came along, after eighteen years of marriage, some of their passion had cooled, but their commitment had not, which I discovered at the overconfident age of fifteen.

I asked Dad's permission to attend a party at a friend's house. He adamantly refused and warned me not to leave the house. I was angry that he'd taken such a firm stance and said to mom, "I don't need his permission. I'm very capable of making my own decisions, and I'm going anyway."

Mom responded with reproof. "Your dad loves you; you will obey him and not disrespect him under any circumstances. God will punish you if you rebel against your dad."

That was a defining moment: I realized how committed Mom was to Dad. She understood his love and had his back. Somehow, I'd ignored lessons about their love and relied on the lessons I'd learned from my favorite stars, which was more entertaining.

In the meantime, Mom kept me busy in the church to steer me away from trouble. She believed that an idle mind was the devil's workshop. My parents hired a musician, who performed live shows on the Las Vegas Strip to give me weekly piano lessons at home. After several years of formal training and classical music lessons, I was appointed choir director at our church. Church became a way of life for me. I was not permitted to hang out with my typical teenage peers. If I wasn't in school, I was in church, participating in weekly Bible study, prayer services, and Sunday and Wednesday church services. Church, however, did not deter the interest of young men, as Mother Nature would have it. I recall, during street ministry, how young men cruised by in their cars, flirting while I sat in the back of a pickup truck playing songs of worship on a Hammond organ. Mom and church were my guardians, often reminding me not to cast my pearls before swine, lest they trample upon them. My jewels were mine to protect until marriage, and so I did. However, like women characters in the love movies, I was naïve and innocent, and didn't understand what real love looked like. I believed the fairy-tale version that my knight in shining armor would ride in on a white horse to claim his princess. The only action required on my part was to be beautiful, charming, and wait for love to happen.

Moment of Reflection

My exposure to a fairy-tale version of love on television had a major effect on the very core of my belief system. Like the part of an iceberg that is hidden beneath the surface of the water, it influenced the course of my life and the decisions I made in choosing mates. My parents showed their commitment to each other, but their love relationship was a mystery to me during my impressionable years. Love was not talked about at home or at church in such a way that I could learn the important lessons that would affect my choices about love and marriage. God teaches us, "Keep thy heart with all diligence; for out of it are the issues of life" (Proverbs 4:23 KJV). I didn't understand this in my youth and relied on a shallow, fairy-tale version of love that would later cause me years of disappointment and grief.

CHAPTER 2

Love in the Wilderness

Cursed is the man who trusts in man and makes flesh is strength, whose heart departs from the Lord.

—Jeremiah 17:5 KJV

As a young woman I felt empowered and at the same time frightened by the attention I was receiving from men. Security came through the eyes of the church. In my second year of college, I married a minister at the tender age of twenty-one with all the hopes and dreams of loving someone for a lifetime. He was the one, I thought, worthy of my "jewels," which I had preserved for this important occasion. I reveled in the idea that he was mature, grounded in his Christian faith, and understood the commitment that comes with love and marriage. He had chosen me as his wife, and I believed that we had a solid foundation on which to build a lasting relationship. As real life happened, the promise "to love and to cherish, till death do us part" was broken. After eighteen months of marriage I was facing divorce and single parenthood.

Devastated, I blamed God and the church for my failed marriage. After the divorce, the church asked me to continue God's work as the director over the music ministry. I served for a while, but I felt spiritually disconnected. Disillusioned and no longer able to carry the burden of disappointment, I took a sabbatical from God's service. I recall having this heartfelt conversation with God, which led to many years in the wilderness trying to find my way.

"God, I'm hurting and disappointed. Why did this have to happen to me? The pain is too much to bear. I'm leaving the church because I have too much respect to serve you under false pretenses. Please forgive me for this action. I ask that You not forget me and that You find a way to bring me back someday. I'm leaving for now."

In my mind, God took a backseat, and anger, disappointment, and loneliness became unwelcome companions, which led to my decision to give myself a helping hand. Entering into the wilderness of love was no easy task. I had been under the protection of God, family, and church, which was deeply ingrained in my heart. Disconnected from God and the body of Christ, I returned to college to complete my teaching degree and met an energetic young man, a fellow student. I became intrigued by his intelligence, entrepreneurial spirit, and eloquent conversation that convinced me we could have a bright future together. I welcomed the attention I was receiving from him, which gave me the boost of self-esteem I so desperately needed. My failed marriage had shaken my confidence and self-image, and I had begun to believe that I was not woman enough to sustain a marriage with a man. This young man made me feel wanted, and embraced the responsibility of being a father to my daughter. I thought to myself, a life with him couldn't possibly be any worse than my marriage; He's a family- and community-minded person with integrity and moral character. The spiritual aspects of my Christian life took a backseat as I opened my heart once again and accepted his proposal of marriage.

During the course of our marriage, we had two beautiful children. He became a doting father who loved his children and his wife. As life happened again, we were faced with the challenge of sustaining the relationship while struggling to resolve financial, parenting, and relationship issues without having a foundation of spiritual unity to stand on. I had walked away from my relationship with God and did not feel worthy of asking Him to intervene on our behalf. My husband and I sought answers to our problems, but like a roller coaster spiraling down, we could not change the direction our marriage had taken. I felt defeated as the chasm between us grew wider and we grew further apart. The foundation we built our relationship on was not enough to sustain the marriage, and again I was facing divorce, after fifteen years of marriage.

I sought answers to understand why I had failed at love twice. Once again, I had opened my heart with the intentions of loving one person for a lifetime, but this had not become my reality. The failure of two marriages, the first one under the eyes of the church and the second one on my own terms, had left me bitter, disheartened, and in despair. I felt like the mistakes I had made were irreparable and I blamed myself for the direction my life had taken. Feeling unable to redeem myself, I decided to take a different pathway to understand the roles that men and women play in relationships. I took on the task of seeking to find out what I was doing wrong by researching self-help books and magazine articles, and talking with so-called experts on the subject of love, with the goal in mind of making myself more appealing and capable of sustaining a relationship with a man. I attributed my failure, in part, to a lack of experience in the selection process, and I wanted no more surprises in my choice of a mate. I rationalized that with insight, ingenuity, and appeal, I could influence the outcome of a relationship by making wise choices and acting responsibly to attract a suitable mate. My thinking shifted from waiting for love to happen to seeking out someone to make love happen with.

After a readjustment period, I was ready to venture out again and decided to try dating. The decision was uncomfortable for me, as I had little experience in matters of dating and was not as innocent and trusting of others as I had been previously. I had experienced pain and disappointment and did not want to travel down that road again. What was equally important to me was protecting my children from unsavory characters in pursuit of love, which I attributed to the way my parents had raised me during my earlier years. It was important that I meet someone who was trustworthy, whom I could trust to have a productive relationship with my children as well.

While waiting to join a group of friends to attend a concert, I met a friendly gentleman who introduced himself and offered me a drink in a nonthreatening way. Intrigued by his maturity and politeness, I accepted his offer. His at-a-glance qualities and conversation appeared to be a good match for my wits, and I suggested we exchange phone numbers to keep in touch, to which he agreed. Several days passed before I decided to make that first call. This bold move on my part was out of character for me, but I anxiously made the call and was pleased when he responded with interest in a casual and polite way. I felt better about my bold move the next day, when he initiated a return call. We'd made a connection by sharing common experiences, which created the foundation for our friendship. Over time, we found solace in talking and sharing our lives as the relationship evolved into something more intimate.

Envisioning what our lives could be like together took precedence in my mind while I overlooked obvious signs of discord that were evident as the relationship evolved. I was blinded by my strong desire for a mate, and I wanted him. I thought I could convince this man that I was the perfect match for him. I was up for the challenge of becoming an "essential person" in his life without a marriage contract for a period of time. The relationship fulfilled our desires for companionship for many years as we enjoyed extravagant vacations, friends, and family, and celebrated holidays. What's very interesting is that during the course of the relationship, it was never clear to me whether we wanted similar outcomes.

As time passed, I begin to initiate conversations about our future to decide if marriage was an option for us, which ended abruptly with moments of uncomfortable silence and left a painful, gut-wrenching feeling of rejection I refused to acknowledge. However, I wasn't ready to walk away, because I enjoyed the benefits of companionship and feared being alone.

I was in denial of my feelings about the unspoken rejection and lied to convince myself that he loved me but needed more time to commit. Disappointed, I began to settle for less than what I desired and was unwilling to face the reality that I was living a dream not shared. I was casting my pearls to someone who did not want to claim them on a long-term basis. I was a well-treated lover as long as I did not make any demands on the future of the relationship. I strived to maintain a calm, peaceful existence, but "playing house" did not sit well with me. Even though I had departed from the Lord, I knew this was not the way God intended men and women to live, and therefore, I became restless with the terms of the relationship.

There were opportunities when I thought I should abandon the relationship, but multiple events happened that influenced my decision to stay. For many years, I willingly took on the roles of lover, nurturer, cook, nursemaid, and analyst and became his shoulder to cry on, thinking that my good deeds would not go unnoticed and would prove that I was worthy of his love.

The relationship ebbed and flowed for years with troubled waters brewing beneath the surface. I buried what I knew to be true in my heart and settled on a vague promise of marriage.

It was in the ninth year when the relationship became what I had envisioned it should be. He gave me an engagement ring with a promise to wed. *Finally,* I thought, *I've met the one person to love for a lifetime,* but then I noticed the hesitation in his willingness to make definite wedding plans. We started to spend less time together, traveling in different directions with our lives and interests. He was pulling away, and the closeness between us began to deteriorate as our wedding plans unraveled. Out of fear that he was distancing himself from the relationship, I asked him if he still wanted to marry me. Finally, the moment of truth arrived when he spoke what my heart had known all along: "No," he said. "If I had to give you one reason why I should not marry you, I do not have one. I just do not want to marry you."

He no longer wanted to continue the relationship; he was ready to move on, and so he did. Painfully, I realized that he had never been mine to have; He had gladly given me material things, out of convenience, but had never agreed to give me himself. As devastated as I was, realizing this cold, hard truth began my process of healing and returning to God's fold. I had tried to make love happen for me, and I had failed.

Moment of Reflection

We often compromise who we are and our relationship with God to seek a mate on our own. Women often believe that they can change the mind of a man by manipulating a situation. Out of desperation, I chose to believe that I had not been successful at love because I had not met the right person. My fantasy unraveled in time, bringing emotional pain that brought me to my knees. We become impatient and at times lack the spiritual guidance needed to stay connected with God. My emotions and beliefs (hurt, anger, loneliness, and abandonment) led me down a pathway that took me further away from what God desired for me. We lose trust in knowing He has our best interests at heart. As I reflect, I thank God that He loved me enough to disrupt my plans to marry. I had lost all joy and happiness, and I realized at this point that I was broken inside and needed a personal relationship with God to find peace. I had to reclaim my place in God's kingdom.

CHAPTER 3

Forgive and Let Go

"For I know the thoughts that I think toward you," saith the Lord, "thoughts of peace, and not of evil, to give you an expected end."

—Jeremiah 29:11 KJV

The breakup of the nine-year relationship left me in a state of crisis. The pain from the rejection was so intense, it felt like huge claws gripping my heart in a stronghold, suffocating me and cutting off any relief from painful emotions, thoughts, and feelings. I looked in the mirror at my swollen face and eyes, which were wrought with tears and great sadness. My heart was broken; I had caused the pain, and promised myself never to return to that place of grief again. I couldn't eat, drink, or sleep for weeks on end, and was mentally exhausted from all the grieving and succumbed to illness after the breakup.

My mind constantly revisited the painful memories of rejection, and I was unable to break this cycle of mental torture. I would awake in the middle of the night with nightmares. My heart would be palpitating and my mind racing, wanting to escape from my present state, but there was nowhere to go. I was constantly anxious about seeing him in the community during this fragile state of existence. Reaching out to friends and family did not lessen my grief. I looked into the faces of my children, whose lives had been affected by the breakup, and saw disappointment and hurt, knowing trust had been broken. They hated to see their mom in a state of despair. I tried to shelter them from the pain I was feeling, but they intuitively knew what I was going through and stayed by my side during my darkest moments.

Feeling the sting of rejection, I also felt heavily condemned for abandoning a relationship with God that came through the traditional eyes of the church and my family. I thought I knew what it meant to be a follower of Christ, but this was the first time that He had intervened and made His presence known to me in a way I had never experienced. God wanted a personal relationship with me. I grieved deeply and sought His forgiveness. Not deserving of God's grace, I needed His love and again I say, His forgiveness. Remorseful about the offense I had caused Him, I cried out to Him as I lay listless on the floor with tears streaming down my face, praying the prayer of forgiveness. I also sought comfort in reading the Bible and listening to spiritual songs over and over again.

I had walked away from God, but He had not walked away from me. In the midst of the storm, I heard His voice. "You will have no other God before me. I'm a jealous God." I prayed to get my joy and peace back and came to realize that I could not do it alone. I knew within my heart that revenge for the rejection I felt was not in order, because I had been operating in the flesh, outside of God's will, for many years. In spite of the pain and disappointment, God instructed me to let go of the relationship.

I cried out and asked God to usher me through my storm. He heard my cry and began to manifest His love in ways that brought direction and promise. On a Sunday afternoon, I fell asleep on the patio swing, and saw a vision of a garden: The garden was vibrant with color and had a brick pathway that meandered through lush green plants. There was a stream of water running freely under a bridge that crossed over to middle ground where a blooming cherry blossom tree stood. As I looked up, I saw other varieties of trees, some with limbs hanging to the ground in variations of green and autumn hues. A pagoda was among the ground-cover plants near some big yellow roses. The peaceful surroundings in this place were beautiful.

This vision had a major effect on me. As I opened my eyes, I was assured that in the midst of the storm, all would be well. That evening, a seed of hope was planted in my heart. Even today, I have a great love for gardens.

One of the assignments God gave me was to write a letter of forgiveness. It was not easy to forgive someone who had hurt me so deeply, but there was a lesson He wanted me to learn. It was a tall order, but I knew I had to obey God if I was going to be healed. In the letter I wrote the following:

I abandoned my relationship with God in pursuit of a relationship outside of God's will. Through God's grace He reconciled me to Himself and asked me to extend grace and forgiveness to you as He has extended His to me. Jesus loves us both and wishes that neither us would perish, as He gave His life that we might be saved. I encourage you to secure a personal relationship with God so that you may have peace and eternal life. I only wish you the best of what God desires for your life.

With a painful heart, I sent the letter, but forgiveness did not come right away. I recalled having a conversation with God: "Lord, how can I forgive this man while I'm in such pain and still hurting?" His response was "I forgave you and others who persecuted me. It hurts me to see men reject me daily, but I continue to extend grace so that they might be saved. I'm not interested in destroying man but in saving mankind." This became a turning point in my ability to forgive and let go. I realized that as long as man is operating in the flesh and does not have a relationship with God, he will disappoint himself and others, offering only what he possesses, whether good or bad. I was asking this man to give me what he could not deliver. This man was hurting himself and was in no position to give me the relationship I desired. My anger began to turn into compassion and understanding.

I spent a lot of time in solitude with God during this period. While I was seeking God's help, my broken heart was not completely mended. During the healing process, I continued to experience bouts of loneliness and sadness. Many nights, I would curl up and wrap my arms around my body, asking God for comfort and peace. I could feel the warmth of God's presence as He enabled me to drift off into a peaceful sleep. One of those nights, I drifted off to sleep and dreamed this dream:

I entered my home and placed my car keys and purse on the table by the sofa. Above the table was a beautiful picture of me with a man I'd never seen before. Realizing I was not alone, I proceeded to the bedroom. Eager to see who this man was, I entered the bedroom and found him lying in bed beneath the covers. As I pulled back the covers to see the man's face, I realized that the man in my bed was Jesus himself.

I awoke from this dream realizing that I had not totally committed to my relationship with God and was holding on to past desires. I had a lesson to learn. God would not allow another person to enter my life until I learned to totally embrace and depend on Him. He had to be first in my life. Only then would I be able to completely and totally let go of the past. The warmth of God's presence continued, and my rest became more and more peaceful over time. As I embraced my relationship with God, He began to manifest His love and care in ways that inspired me to write. One morning, as I was exercising on the treadmill, tears began to fall down my face as I felt God's presence in the room. Later that morning, I began to write words God spoke to my heart; I call it a "love letter" from God.

> With no regrets, I give myself freely.
> Accept the depth, scope, and breadth of my love,
> No strings attached.
> Waiting patiently for your return
> For you to embrace me, to trust me,
> For I love you—yes, you—in the truest form.
> I know your comings and goings.
> I've counted every hair on your head.

I've seen your tears in the night.
Holding you in my arms to comfort you,
My only desire is to give you hope
And a life full of joy.
I've seen your unsettling thoughts,
Have felt your attention toward others.
Jealous as I might be,
I wait patiently for your return.
Will you embrace me? Will you trust me?
For I love you—yes, you—in the truest form.
I've sacrificed all that I have.
Painful as rejection may be,
It does not change the love I have for you.
I promise to carry you through life's seasons,
For my love is constant in its truest form.
I'll never leave you for another,
Neither will death do us part,
For our love is eternal
Only if you're willing
To embrace me, trust me,
For I love you—yes, you—in the truest form.

Moment of Reflection

The pain I created, doing it my way and giving myself a hand, was greater than any pain I had ever experienced before. It was as if Satan had plans to destroy me, but because of God's love, He intervened. His correction did not feel good to my flesh, but I was His, and He was reconciling me to Himself. God tells us in Isaiah 55:8–9 (KJV), "For my thoughts are not your thoughts, neither are your ways my ways, saith the Lord. For as the heavens are higher than the earth, so are my ways higher than your ways, and my thoughts than your thoughts."

God wasn't going to allow me travel down a path that would steer me away from His purpose for my life. God cared, and because of His care, He changed my course. During this healing process, He guided me through forgiveness, which did not come easily, but there was an important lesson for me to learn. I had to trust where God wanted to take me and knew there wouldn't be room for baggage. I had to forgive and let go. I planted a serenity garden as a reminder of the promise God made to give me a future of hope and promise. In the midst of my garden, a plaque reads, "Be still and know that I am God!"

CHAPTER 4

Fellowship and Friends

He restoreth my soul; he leads me in the paths of righteousness for His name's sake.

—Psalm 23:3 KJV

After months of solitude, I decided to attend a new church in the community, which was an important step for me. The relationship with my previous church had soured and left me bitter after my first failed marriage. The quiet time I had spent with God helped me understand where I had been misguided. Being director over the music ministry early on had not been enough to sustain me. I needed a close personal relationship with God.

I was eager to hear the message of salvation and to be reconciled to God's fold. As I stood at the back of the church, a guest minister was preaching the message of prosperity. The members of the congregation were ecstatic with praise as they received prophetic messages of financial wealth. My heart sank in disappointment. I needed to hear the message of salvation, and like the prodigal son returning to his father's house, I wanted to return to my heavenly Father's house. I started to leave but decided to stay. I went home disappointed but decided to go back one more time because the pastor, who had been out of town, would be returning the following Sunday.

Upon my second visit, the pastor delivered a message of salvation and God's love, which was spiritual food for my soul. It felt good to be among fellow worshippers again after years in the wilderness. While sitting in the service, I noticed the presence of an old friend from the past.

Shirley was sitting four rows in front of me. I hadn't seen her since we were children, but I knew, from the silhouette of her head, that it was her. I recalled our childhood years, and how we would sit on the stairs of her front porch cutting out paper dolls and playing house. In the alley behind our homes, we would join with the neighborhood kids to play baseball using whatever materials we could find: a scrap of lumber for a bat, spray paint to mark the bases, a baseball, and a catcher's mitt.

Our mothers had been friends and served on the Women's Auxiliary Board at church. My dad would share hunting and fishing stories with her dad when he returned home from a hunting trip with a deer hanging off the back of his pickup truck. We would watch as Dad dressed out the deer that hung from a clothesline pole in the back alley before taking it to the local deer-processing company. Our fathers were hunters, and we grew up on what they brought to the table to eat.

We celebrated the Fourth of July with barbecues, fireworks, and Mom's homemade, old-fashioned vanilla ice cream and butter pound cake. At nightfall, we would settle on the lawn to watch the city fireworks light up the sky above downtown's neon lights. Our friendship had been interrupted when Shirley moved from the neighborhood. Mom took me to visit a few times, but after a while, we lost contact. I remember the sadness I felt at losing my best friend.

As the church congregation emptied into the parking lot, I called her name. She turned and recognized me at a glance. Seeing her again, it was as if something comfortable and familiar had returned. At this time in my life, I needed her friendship. As it turned out, she was involved in the counseling ministry, and through her friendship we created a fellowship of close girlfriends.

We would plan gatherings to enjoy a home-cooked southern meal, which often consisted of greens, corn bread, chicken, yams, potato salad, cake, and/or banana pudding for dessert. Our emotional and spiritual bond grew as we shared the most intimate stories of our lives. We had tried marriage, dating, and the club scene to find love and had failed. We had become single parents and knew happiness did not lie in the way we had lived our lives. The anchors of our lives were now our faith in God and our friendship. We prayed, danced, laughed, and sometimes cried together, leaning on each other for support. We were learning to value who we are in Christ, learning to trust God, and understand what God's love really looked like for His children. I often referred to our time spent together as Girlfriend Call sessions that sometimes extended into the next morning with breakfast. We began to hold monthly gatherings, defining our social network and entertainment with an intimate circle of girlfriends.

My heartbreak, once felt so deeply, began to take a backseat as God began to restore my joy. I was able to laugh again and make plans for my life that took on a new direction. Anxieties that I'd felt as a result of the breakup began to subside. I found myself thinking less about memories and more about living in the moment. Although my friends talked openly about wanting love and marriage, I wasn't ready to open my heart to consider the possibility of making a life with someone else, because I was still in the process of emotionally healing. I had become protective of my heart and did not feel that I could trust enough to love again. I was happy to have their friendship and support, but I was not ready for companionship. I had made an ungodly choice of mates that had a lingering effect I needed to overcome.

As part of God's plans for my life, He began to deal with my heart about my music. When I had walked away from God's service, I had also placed my music on the back burner for many years. The piano my parents bought for me, at the age of nine, now resided in my home collecting dust. I recalled having this recurring dream about my music. I would sit down to play the piano but could no longer hear the sound of the ivory keys. The dream disturbed me for some time until one day a friend approached me with a message from God to return to my music. One night as I was sleeping, I dreamed that I was battling spirits of darkness as they attacked me with great force. I fought back with tenacity, unwilling to yield, calling out to God for protection. As I began to quote God's word—"though I walk through the valley of the shadow of death, I will fear no evil for thou art with me"—the spirits of darkness left. What then appeared before me was a host of angels. They began to sing a beautiful song of praise that I'd never heard before. In a semiconscious state, I asked the angel to allow me to remember the song when I awoke. My request was granted. As I awoke from a deep slumber at 2:30 a.m., the words and melody of the song were resonating in my heart. I arose quickly and stumbled to the piano to play out the melody and write the words down. I knew that if I did not act quickly, the blessing would be lost forever.

These visitations of hearing angelic songs of praise continue to happen from time to time. Now I keep a recorder by my bed to capture the words and melody of angelic songs I hear when I'm sleeping. Music has become so much a part of my relationship with God that I awake with songs of praise in my heart on a regular basis. My music has become such an intimate connection between God and me that I also share it with family and friends.

Moment of Reflection

As the period of solitude came to a close, it was God's plan for me to establish friendships with fellow Christians for spiritual support. They became a vital part of my healing as the pain of loss began to subside and my life took on new meaning in a different direction. I no longer felt isolated in my grief. Oftentimes, we isolate ourselves from our Christian brothers and sisters when we are experiencing trials and tribulations. This creates an opportunity for Satan to attack, as he is a predator. And like a predator, he will attack when you are vulnerable and alone, leading you into hopelessness and despair.

My previous friends, who were associated with the failed relationship, were not able to console me, because they did not have answers. They themselves were in dark places and struggled to make sense of their lives through whatever means they could find. I totally disassociated myself from these acquaintances, as I found no pleasure in socializing with them. Like a fish out of water, I was no longer able to fit into their circles. As it says in 2 Corinthians 6:17 KJV, God was requiring me to "come out from among them and be ye separate" for His purposes. My answers to love and marriage were not to be found through the constructs of the world.

 CHAPTER 5

Restoration

Trust in the Lord with all thine heart; and lean not unto thine own understanding. In all thy ways acknowledge him, and he shall direct thy paths.

—Proverbs 3:5–6 KJV

God had a greater plan for my life, ushering me through my most difficult moments with love and guidance. My fragile heart was mending as He began to replace sadness with joy and attended to my personal needs in very intimate ways I never could have imagined. I was visiting Sandra in Alabama when we decided, on the spur of the moment, to visit Florida with friends. As I stood on the balcony of our condo, overlooking the sandy beach of the Pensacola coast, tears of joy began to swell in my eyes. I realized that I was in this beautiful place the same week of the year that I would have been enjoying the sandy beaches of the Baja coast of Mexico with my previous mate. This was an unexpected event where God was demonstrating His love in a profound way. He was speaking to my heart: "Trust me; I am the source for all that you desire." I felt God's presence and knew I was not alone; He was giving me the assurance of His love.

God continued to restore and instruct me on matters of health, parenting, career choices, and yes, money matters. I witnessed God's blessings in my children's lives as well. They were able to attend fine universities and receive their educations while we lived on a shoestring budget. I often tell others that if I had to explain how this task was accomplished, being a single parent on a teacher's salary, I couldn't explain it, and it wouldn't make sense when you add up the dollar amount.

There was no earthly explanation for it all. God was caring for me as a man would care for a loving wife and family.

I was driving home from a church event one Saturday afternoon when I saw a new housing development in the far distance. I felt a strong need to tour the homes, but my initial thought was *I can't afford to buy a house*, so I continued on toward my destination. However, I couldn't seem to let go of the idea that God was guiding me to tour the homes. I made a U-turn and drove through the neighborhood, admiring the new development. I noticed that several families had moved into their homes, whereas other houses were still under construction. Two streets of vacant lots were marked for future construction to build on according to a new buyer's specifications. Again, I told myself, *You can't afford to buy one of these houses*. Listening to practical reasoning, I left the development and had continued toward my destination when the Lord spoke a second time: "Go back and tour the models." When I returned and entered the homes, one of the models caught my attention. I knew it was for me. It was what I had envisioned and desired for many years. Two days later, I signed a contract to have the home built. There were additional builder's options that I wanted, but I was unable to finance them up front. During the building phase, the builder decided to reduce the amount of the down payment required for options, which allowed me to "have my cake and eat it too." Within a month of moving into my new home, I received a salary increase. There was a contractual change in my employment, and a year later, I got a promotion. God made provisions beyond what I could ever have imagined. I have lived in and enjoyed this home for many years with minimal debt. Not once have I had to stress about the payments. Again I say there is no earthly explanation for it.

God also began to instruct me in the area of self-control, an attribute of the spirit I had disregarded. He directed me on matters of spending and functionality as my shopping became more purposeful and focused. One day, I wanted to purchase custom-made window treatments for my new home. I was flipping through a catalog looking at window treatments when I felt God speaking to my heart, saying, "No, you can make them yourself. You have the skill; use it." Not confident about the outcome, I purchased the raw materials and was able to make beautiful window coverings for the first time in my life. God wanted me to be a good steward of His blessings by using the talent He had blessed me with.

Lacking self-control, I had gained an exorbitant amount of weight over the years, which had begun to affect my health. With a diagnosis of type-2 diabetes and high blood pressure, I needed a lifestyle change, as my weight had been fluctuating for many years. Struggling with my consumption of food, I would diet for a season but oftentimes resort to eating comfort foods that were harmful to my health. I mentally coped with my disappointment by making excuses, saying, "I'm big boned, and I naturally carry more muscle weight than fat weight." Although some of that was true, I was making excuses and compromising the quality of life the Lord wanted me to have. I had come to a place where I did not feel good and did not like my self-image as I looked at my imperfections staring back at me in the mirror. I was embarrassed and came to believe that a man would not accept and love me in my current physical state. However, I could not find the discipline to break the cycle of eating while loathing myself at the same time. I also noticed, over time, that my doctor was increasing the number of pills I was taking to prevent the onset of debilitating diseases. I knew I was headed for trouble when, during a doctor's visit, I received a wakeup call. The doctor said firmly, "You have type-2 diabetes and need insulin to get your blood sugar under control; your vital organs, limbs, and vision could be negatively impacted if you continue to eat the way you are eating." This doctor's report placed fear in my heart; I could no longer ignore the obvious signs, as my mother and grandmother had suffered and died from strokes and heart failure. The odds were against me, and I was teetering on the edge of a health crisis.

Many nights, I would wake up around 2:00 a.m. in the still quietness of early morning with gut-wrenching fear, thinking, *If I don't change my ways, I will die before my time.* I prayed, "Lord, I need your help. I can't do this alone! I'm struggling and scared. I want change for a better life, but I can't do it by myself. Please show me a better way."

My daughter joined a weight loss program and asked me to join with her. I had tried this program before and discontinued it, but I had had earlier success with weight loss. As the story goes, the weight loss was short lived, and I had gradually gained back what I had lost, plus more. After a year of procrastination, I decided to return. My pride had gotten in the way of admitting my failure, which was another cold, painful reality for me. In the process of accepting this reality, my mind-set began to change as I learned new ways to prepare foods, make more healthful choices, exercise, and let go of old eating habits. There were moments when I grieved for the foods that I loved; I was experiencing an emotional death of my old ways of eating in exchange for a healthier lifestyle.

It seemed that everywhere I went, food was ever present to sabotage the direction I was taking. I realized the program was not enough to sustain my efforts. I needed spiritual support. God intervened and showed me how to bury my old eating habits, enjoy the natural bounty of healthful foods, and most of all, learn to say, "No, thank you" and make conscientious choices about what goes on my plate. There were times my weight loss stagnated and I would become anxious. God would advise me to "Relax and enjoy the journey. Time is needed for this transformation to sustain the change you desire." Over time, my eating habits improved, and learning to say no became easier. God has been my true partner in living a more healthful lifestyle, and I'm enjoying the benefits of a better quality of life with restful nights, high energy, and a reduction in medications.

Moment of Reflection

God was concerned not only about my spiritual walk, but also about my overall well-being in the most intimate way. My fragile state of existence faded away. I became more confident and self-assured in His care. There was a three-year period of lessons when I had to learn to trust God. Time and time again, He proved His faithfulness through tangible deeds. God's constant attention to the details of my personal life ruled out any chance that these occurrences were happening by coincidence. No one could have forecast these events, and money did not limit what God wanted me to have. I was being restored, yet there were more lessons for me to learn.

CHAPTER 6

Waiting

> But let patience have her perfect work, that ye may be perfect and entire, wanting nothing.
>
> —James 1:4 KJV

Patience was not an easy lesson to learn as God attended to my needs with persistence and care. The fact remained that in my heart, I still wanted a sustained love and marriage with a man. Time with God helped me manage the ebb and flow of my emotions, but I could never totally rid myself of the frustration that came with waiting. There were periods of silence where I did not hear from God. Life was good, but material things had lost their luster, and shopping for more stuff became mundane. I felt as though I was living in a vacuum in a home with beautiful surroundings but with only the sound of my thoughts. I began to feel tired and worn in the process of waiting. I carried on many conversations with God, repeatedly requesting companionship. I knew God was hearing my prayers, but I wanted to know why He was not answering me. I started bargaining conversations with God: "If it is your plan for me to remain single for the rest of my life, please grant me complete peace and contentment in this area, as I've been waiting for a long time." I was not alone in experiencing these moments of frustration; my girlfriends also struggled with the desire for companionship. At times, one of us would issue a distress call for a Girlfriend Call session. We would gather and pray to provide an anchor of support for each other.

During this waiting period, I experienced moments of anxiety, loneliness, and isolation with a desire to be loved. My husband was not materializing fast enough. I recalled noticing the attention of men who initiated no more than a hello with a smile without an "I want to get to know you better" conversation. It seemed as though there was a shield of protection around me they chose not to penetrate. This happened so often that I wondered what they were thinking and why I was not capturing their attention in a meaningful way. As frustration set in again, temptation reared its ugly head, and I began to compromise my relationship with the Lord and the lessons He had taught me earlier. During one of these moments of frustration, I decided to go to a club to hear a band on a Saturday night. I was sitting in a dark corner of the club as partygoers drank and danced to the sound of R&B and Soul Jams. As I sat there, the Lord brought conviction with these words: "What are you doing here? You know better." I left in tears, realizing that I could not disregard the love and correction I had received from Him. I was toying with temptation and seeking to fulfill my emotional and physical needs out of sheer frustration from the process of waiting.

Again, I cried out to the Lord for relief and comfort. I wanted to live in contentment with my singleness and did not want to waver in my Christian walk. While visiting California,

I confided in my sister about my struggle. As we joined in prayer, God confirmed through her that He had not forgotten about me and that in due time, He would fulfill my desire for love. A second confirmation came late one evening when I was walking across the parking lot of a restaurant. Out of nowhere, a man and a woman approached me and asked if they could pray for me. For reasons I can't explain, I accepted their offer because I believed there was a reason I had met them and that their intervention was the hand of God. I shared with them that my father had passed recently and several days before his death, he had expressed his desire for me to have someone to love. We stood in the parking lot and prayed, when the man proceeded to tell me that God had chosen a mate for me. It was not yet his time to come into my life, because he was overcoming a personal challenge in his own life, but God would bring us together in the right season.

These moments of confirmation began to ease my frustration as I was assured that God had not forgotten about me. Confirmation also came in the form of a dream I had: I was sitting on a large boulder on top of a summit overlooking Lake Tahoe, surrounded by tall pine trees, when a tall, dark, handsome man approached me. He began to sing a song so intimate that it captured the essence of my heart. It was as if the song was written just for me with the perfect mix of words, progression, and melody. Oh, the man knew me well; no instructions were needed, and no explanation was required. God gently spoke these words to my heart: "Be still, when he comes, he will know your song." Awakening from the dream, I realized I was not waiting in vain; I had to totally surrender all my anxiety, loneliness, and frustration and honor God's timing.

One Saturday evening as I sat alone at home playing the piano, God instructed me to get busy with ministry and not focus on what I did not have. He had blessed me with the gift of music and wanted me to bless others; it was not His intention for me to enjoy it in a vacuum. For a season, I joined a group of fellow worshippers to provide music on Sunday at a rehabilitation facility for Alzheimer's patients who came from different walks of life. I could tell by their appearance that they were struggling to hold on to important events of their lives that were fading because of memory loss. Hymns that meant a lot to them were carefully selected to encourage them to sing along. One of their favorite hymns was "Jesus Loves Me" written by Anna Bartlett Warner in the 1900s, and it was easy for them to sing along. I didn't realize how much the music meant to them until one Sunday when I thought to myself, *I'm going to stay home and rest.* When I returned the following Sunday, the patients surprised me by wanting to know why I had not been there; they had missed the music and singing. It was an awakening experience to realize that what I had to offer was important to them. What they didn't realize was that they were teaching me a lesson of patience and love as I took my eyes off of my circumstances and focused on their needs. I began to look forward to Sunday's ministry because I needed their fellowship as much as they needed mine. I felt that I was in the right place; God was using me for His purpose through worship and praise. The fellowship continued to grow as more patients arrived early in preparation for Sunday services.

I asked my sisters in Christ, who also participated in the fellowship service, if they would pray with me: I wanted to ask God for a husband, which required me to put aside my pride before God and my Christian sisters. Although I had desired a husband, I had neglected to make an official request. In Matthew 18:19 (KJV), God's word says "that if two of you shall agree on earth as touching any thing that they shall ask, it shall be done for them of my Father which is in heaven." I had come to realize that this was an important step in my walk of faith with God fulfilling His promise. As we prayed, another sister also came forward with her request for a mate; I realized then that I was not alone.

Several months later, my girlfriend, sister, and I decided to take a summer vacation to Europe. One of the highlights of our trip was a visit to the monastery at Montserrat, a mountain retreat and popular pilgrimage destination for many in the Catalonia area of Spain. I had learned about the monastery while watching an episode on places to travel, which piqued my interest and desire to visit. Three years later, there I was, standing in that place. No media could do justice to the real experience of being there. The views from the top of the mountain range looking downward were spectacular and breathtaking, with beautiful vineyards winding down one side of the mountain. It was as if the mountains stood in silence out of reverence for God's greatness.

As my traveling partners and I approached the entrance to the basilica, we were welcomed by large stone sculptures of Jesus and the twelve disciples, intricately carved into the mountain above the entrance. We felt serenity and peace in this place in such a profound way that it brought tears to our eyes. With reverence and gratitude, I looked into my friend's eyes and commented, "God really does exist and cares for us, and we have to trust Him totally." At that moment, I realized the greatness of God's presence and the effect He's had on the world, which is greater than I had ever imagined.

My spiritual connection with God became more intimate while meandering through crowds of people in Venice, walking through corridors that opened up to St. Mark's Square. As I was crossing over a cobblestone bridge, my heart cried out to God with remorse and gratitude. "Lord, thank you for loving me unconditionally, in spite of my short-comings. What is it you would like for me to do? I surrender all: please use me as an intervention in your service."

Later on that night, we attended a Venetian opera featuring larger-than-life characters dressed in period costumes depicting a story line immersed in tradition, drama, and passion. I didn't understand the lyrics, but the essence of the moment was amazing for reasons I hid from my travel partners at the time. I was experiencing the presence of God.

The air in the room seemed to grow hazy as the sound of the music faded in the background. This phenomenon felt like the presence of the omnipotent, as though God was inside of me, sitting next to me, and present on the stage at the same time. He had my full attention. As the opera proceeded, God spoke to my heart with clarity and precision: "I have not forgotten you. There is much more to come, as I have much greater plans for your life beyond what you can ever imagine."

Several months after I had returned from Europe, I had another dream: I was asked, "Do you believe you will ever marry?" Reflecting on the poor choices I had made in my life and the odds of marrying in my fifties, I responded hesitantly, "My opportunity for love has passed. It's not meant to be. When the voice spoke again, I realized it was an angel. He responded, "No, that is not true. You will marry within two years."

Moment of Reflection

Patience was a difficult but important lesson for me to learn. God had reconciled me to Himself, but there were times when the walk was lonely, when I became distracted and began to lose my spiritual focus. God had made a promise to give me love and marriage, but nothing was happening after eight years of waiting. I got tired and began to doubt and question His intentions. I listened to naysayers who reminded me that "women our age don't marry." Finding a good man was like finding a needle in a haystack, and those who existed were already in committed relationships. I desired to be loved and wanted to be satisfied as I struggled to wait. It was during one of those fragile moments that I began to compromise what God had required of me. However, He did not allow me to travel that same old familiar path that He had delivered me from. He was teaching me patience and trust, and reminded me of my commitment to Him. He understood my struggles, but wanted me to unequivocally surrender all to Him. He was with me while I waited, but wanted me to be spiritually grounded in my relationship with Him first. When faced with the question "Do you believe you will ever marry?" I would have liked to respond with the assurance of God's promise, but the truth is, I wavered in my response. God knew that I had doubt in my heart and had become weary in waiting, but He remained faithful and did not forsake His promise for my life.

CHAPTER 7

The Arrival

> To every thing there is a season, and a time to every purpose under the heaven.
>
> —Ecclesiastes 3:1 KJV

Three months later, my niece, Candice, announced her engagement and wanted the family to meet Thomas. They wanted to marry in Las Vegas and sought my help with wedding arrangements. When they arrived at my home, I noticed how polite and courteous this young man was. He had a pleasant smile and a friendly disposition, but communicated respectfully with very few words. It was difficult for me to tell how Thomas felt about marrying Candice, as I was accustomed to a culture where people were more open in their conversations. When I was alone with Candice, I asked her, "Are you sure Thomas is ready for marriage?" She assured me that he was. What I didn't realize then was that as quiet as Thomas was, he had taken notice of me. I later discovered that when he returned home, he spoke with his dad, saying, "I met my fiancée's aunt, Miss Jackie, who is a very nice lady. The two of you are a lot alike, and I believe she'll be good for you."

Six months later, Candice arrived in Las Vegas along with her wedding party. Arrangements were made for them to stay in a hotel, but Candice decided to stay with me to finalize their wedding plans. The night before the wedding rehearsal, we were discussing the plans when she announced that Thomas' father, Lee, was in town, they had asked him to come to bless their marriage with a prayer. She also proceeded to tell me that she thought we had a lot in common and should meet. I listened as she told me that Lee was a widower, married for thirty-three years until the untimely death of his wife, who had passed five years earlier. I chuckled when I realized that Candice and Thomas were playing Cupid. Previously, I'd had many conversations with Candice about waiting on God to send her the right mate, but I never thought she would be introducing me to someone. They had planned for us to meet but had kept their intentions hidden, without a word spoken, until this time. Thomas' father knew he was coming to bless their marriage, but he also knew it was an opportunity for us to meet.

The day of the wedding rehearsal, a tall, handsome, slender father and his son, Thomas, were standing, side by side, with their hands folded, facing the door as I entered the chapel. Attempting to assume a disposition of calm, I greeted family members as they approached me. Then I sat down and opened my Bible. My assignment was to read a Bible scripture as part of the ceremony, which would be followed by a prayer given by Thomas' father. However, this tactic—appearing preoccupied—wasn't working. I knew his eyes were on me, and I was anxious. I mulled it over in my head, thinking, *Do I speak first or will they walk over to greet me? I don't want to appear forward. Well,* I thought, *since Lee is a guest in town for the first time, let me present myself as friendly and gracious. I don't want to give the wrong impression of being inhospitable.* Father and son had not swayed from their position when I mustered up the courage to introduce myself and invited them to my house, where the family would gather, for the rehearsal dinner. Lee kindly said, "Yes, ma'am" to the dinner invitation with a deep southern drawl that was virile and captivating. He then looked at Thomas, who chuckled in a way that carried a special meaning between them, and said, "I'm going to Miss Jackie's house to eat."

The bride's family stood in the kitchen as Lee and his family arrived at the house for dinner. I could only imagine what Cleopatra and her entourage felt like, meeting Mark Antony for the first time. The first thing I noticed was Lee's cowboy boots and his long legs as I welcomed them to my home.

Although there were obvious differences, there were common threads that tied the two families together as we enjoyed a meal of greens, corn bread, chicken, potato salad, and peach cobbler. Thomas' family had traveled from a southern town surrounded by piney woods, bluebonnets, country roads, and open fields. Candice's family, with southern roots, had migrated in the fifties to the West, which is known for its desert landscape and beautiful mountain ranges, but they had maintained a lifestyle influenced by southern traditions.

Aware of what was occurring I guarded my actions, careful not to send the wrong message. I decided to play gracious hostess, to enjoy the evening with an open heart, no agenda, and no preconceived ideas. As we sat down to eat, Lee asked me, "Do you play the piano?"

"Yes," I answered.

"Will you play and sing for me?" he asked.

I responded, "Yes" again with a smile.

After dinner, my sister, Erma, accompanied me on the piano as we sang. When we began to sing, something wonderful happened; I looked up and saw his heart for the first time: First, he listened, and then he decided to join us in a song. As he stood next to me, we made a spiritual connection. I saw joy in his eyes, peace in his smile, and love in his heart. Although singing was not his strong suit, there was something sensual about his voice and comfortable about his sway. Our hearts experienced a spiritual familiarity that let me know he was secure, strong, caring, and most of all, a man of God who had eyes for me.

The attraction was so obvious that the family took notice as we continued to sing songs of praise. As the evening progressed, we shared stories and enjoyed each other's company with him ever wanting to be in the same room with me as I continued to play gracious hostess.

The next day, when I arrived at the wedding chapel, Lee eagerly met me at the front entrance as I walked up the stairs and commented, "Good morning. You look beautiful." Cupid had shot his arrow at last night's rehearsal dinner, so I had decided to dress to impress him. My girlfriend, Shirley, had come over to my house earlier that morning to lend her advice about what I should wear for the wedding as I eagerly shared with her what had transpired. No time was wasted as Lee asked me for my address and phone number in the presence of my brother, Joe. I noticed the glow in Lee's eyes and felt a little shy as Joe stood there witnessing this event unfold. I wondered what he thought of this man contending for his sister's attention. As the wedding ceremony began, Lee's attention never wavered. He took his place in the wedding procession, next to Thomas, directing intermittent eye contact toward me. I tried not to encourage his eyes-on-me behavior, but the cat was out of the bag. Family members noticed the attention I was receiving as I sat in the front pew, ready to perform the assignment I had been given.

After the wedding ceremony, Lee reached for my hand to sit next to him at the groom's family table, but I declined and explained that special seating was for immediate family members only. However, that did not deter him. He lovingly took my hand again and said, "You are with me." He sat next to me, gently and softly caressing my hand. His conversation was transparent, honest, and uncomplicated. There was no mystery to this man's character as he plainly let his intentions be known. He was a man of God and was wooing me off of my feet. My heart felt as light as a feather floating on thin air. I couldn't stop smiling and giggling inside like a schoolgirl on a first date as others watched in wonderment. I felt appreciated, attractive, and wanted.

Although he didn't know how to dance, he courageously took my hand and followed my lead as we gently swayed to a slow R&B love song. I felt his strength and relished the attention I was receiving. He asked me if I was ready to have a relationship with a man of God who was strong and loving. I responded, "Yes." We paid less attention to the events surrounding us as we engaged in an intimate conversation about love and marriage in the midst of the celebration. We had come to bless Candice's and Thomas' marriage, and in return, God was blessing us.

Moment of Reflection

Lee's unexpected arrival happened as a natural occurrence in God's perfect time. There was no forethought about how it would happen on my part; it just did. Our meeting for the first time was simple and uncomplicated. We made a spiritual connection at the onset of the relationship. There was no need for me to manipulate any turns of events. He knew what he was looking for and initiated the relationship. God instructed me earlier to "Be still: when he comes, he will know your song." And yes, Lee knew my song and played the symphony very well. The protective guard that I had developed from past disappointments disappeared. Like a mother who forgets the pain of labor once her child arrives, I was ready to love again. Falling in love with him was not a choice; love just took its place in my heart. This was definitely the dawn of a new day. Old things were past, and behold, all things were new. Amazing!

CHAPTER 8

The Courtship

> So ought men to love their wives as their own bodies. He that loveth his wife loveth himself.
>
> —Ephesians 5:28 KJV

I received a phone call three days after Lee returned home from Thomas' and Candice's wedding. He had spent time talking with God about the direction He wanted us to take. Lee knew that God had plans for his life and that one day he would be leaving the home he knew. Although several women in his community had expressed interest in him, he knew God had chosen someone special to walk by his side in marriage and ministry.

I picked up the phone and heard his voice as he spoke simple words that brought tears to my eyes: "Hello, Miss Jackie," he said. "The time we spent together was very special. I believe God has brought us together for a purpose. When my wife passed away, I prayed, 'Lord, you wouldn't take love away and not give me another to love.' Miss Jackie, I believe that God has fulfilled His promise, and I believe you are that person to love. I was successful at love and do know how to love. Would you enter into a relationship with me with the intention to marry? I believe that this relationship has God written all over it; He doesn't give his sons and daughters away to just anyone."

My heart was radiating with heat when he ended the conversation with "Good night, darling."

I prayed about his invitation. "Lord, I need to know if this relationship is what You want for me because I don't want to lose my way; I want what You want me to have. If this relationship is not what You want for me, please move this person out of my way." I repeatedly prayed this same prayer over several days until I received God's assurance that this was His doing, which came in a calm and peaceful way. God answered my prayer and I accepted Lee's invitation, and thus began the courtship.

Accepting the invitation brought joy and anxiety. Dating this man of God would differ from what I'd experienced in the wilderness. I was nervous about courting Lee and the differences in our lifestyles. I was accustomed to the entertainment culture of Las Vegas that moved at a fast pace; Lee was accustomed to a relaxed rural town lifestyle. As it turned out, Lee's level of commitment to honoring God's word in matters of dating was as spiritually grounded as mine. He took the lead, as romance filled the air, to establish boundaries that honored his relationship with God and with me. Premarital sex wasn't a consideration; we spent time talking and getting to know each other. Our children often lent advice on dating tips, which didn't always sit well with us. We were building a relationship of trust and communication based on Christian principles.

Lee and I talked on the phone daily as he walked the edge of the piney woods near his home. Sometimes, he would be returning from town and I could hear the sound of his truck as he drove down the red clay road shaded by a canopy of pine, oak, hickory, and sweet-gum trees. Along the edge of the road, wild muscadine and Mustang grapevines grew in bounty along with wildflowers that bordered the barbed-wire fence that led to his home. I would be sitting on my backyard patio 1,400 miles away in Las Vegas, talking to Lee, drinking coffee, and looking at the blue skies that hovered over the jagged-edge mountains. In the background where Lee was, cows were calling in the open field, and a newborn puppy was whimpering as he propped his head on Lee's feet, comforted by the vibration of his deep voice. We lived different lives but shared common ground, which brought a level of maturity to the relationship that made it easy for us to love. Lee was enchanted when I began to send him love poems in the mail, such as this one:

> When God gives you a WOW …
> It stops you in your tracks
> It renders you speechless

Stifles your thoughts

Challenges your beliefs

It changes your course

Creates a paradigm shift

Takes you on a journey

Breathes life into a once-forgotten dream

Changes your appearance

Brings passion to life

Gives peace over unsettling thoughts

Writes a new script to an old story

Gives you a new song for a new day

When God gives you a WOW …

Love had arrived! God had placed it in our hearts, and we were free to love each other. Lee patiently waited to hear from God about our next steps toward matrimony. The courtship would not be drawn out. We knew what we wanted, but we wanted it in God's time. An adjustment period took place, and we began to make room in our lives for each other. Our mind-set changed: we no longer thought as two separate individuals but as one. Lee demonstrated his love with tenderness and quiet strength, displaying affection that was truly adoring, in an old-fashioned kind of way. He told me that when a man loves his wife as Christ loved the church, he should be willing to sacrifice his life for his wife. It took me a while to understand the depth of his love and the level of his commitment. No one had ever told me that they would sacrifice themselves for me. For Lee, love meant giving his all, and he wanted me to have it all. With such commitment, I blossomed, attending to our garden of love with tenderness and care. Peace and satisfaction came in knowing that he loved me, cared for me, and had my best interests at heart.

Moment of Reflection

Words cannot express how I felt when Lee entered my life. All of the preconceived ideas I had about relationships dissipated, as God would not allow me to bring my "baggage" into the courtship. The rules of courtship that I had practiced in the world did not apply to us. We did not do a test run to see if it fit. God brought us together and gave us transparency and direction.

God had instructed me to "Be Still," and I knew that Lee would have to make the first move toward a relationship. In surrendering, I discovered how much he truly appreciated me, and felt loved and adored. For the first time in my life, love was happening the way God intended.

CHAPTER 9

The Proposal

For, lo, the winter is past, the rain is over and gone.

—Solomon 2:11 KJV

The unconventional wedding proposal came in the spring while I was visiting Lee's home. We were attending church services one Sunday morning when Pastor Ron asked Lee to minister to the congregation as the guest speaker. Standing at the podium, Lee asked me to stand and announced to the congregation that I was the woman God had chosen for him to spend the rest of his life with. I listened and thought to myself, *What does this announcement mean? Am I engaged?* I knew we were taking steps toward marriage, but we had not officially discussed our engagement. I pondered on this thought as Lee ministered on how God had sustained him during his struggles, and like Job, restored the love that he had lost. This message gave hope to the congregation, and it became clear to me that there was a divine purpose in God's plan for our lives.

That evening, Lee's children had planned a birthday party for him at the house. Traditionally, birthdays in his family are very important events, an opportunity to celebrate the life of loved ones and friends. Whereas I've struggled with remembering the birthdays of my family, Lee is able to recall birthdays of family members and even old schoolmates with ease. He remembers the birthday of every grandchild in his family and sends them cards on their special day.

Word had spread that I was in town visiting Lee. The community loved Lee and was protective of him as one of their own: a good friend and a loyal family and business man. He lived in the community where his family, for many generations, had raised their children and buried their loved ones. He understood the effect our relationship would have on the community, which I was not aware of, and wanted my introduction to the community to go well. I watched people arrive in cars and trucks, greeting and hugging each other, bringing large containers of food for the celebration. I had cooked some greens and corn bread for the occasion, and watched as women tended to the food in the kitchen and speculated about my cooking ability as Lee's future wife.

Everyone was cordial and polite, in a curious kind of way, but an uneasy quietness settled over the celebration as the crowd gathered in a circle to hear Lee's announcement. He blessed the food, thanked family and friends for attending his birthday celebration, and introduced me as the one whom he had chosen to walk by his side. Few words were spoken; I did not hear one "Congratulations" from those present. From their expressions, I imagined they were wondering, *Who is this woman who is taking Lee away from our community? She is not one of us.*

I began to understand their sense of loss, but I didn't understand why Lee had not discussed our engagement before the announcement. I knew what it all meant, but I needed him to tell me what it meant. That evening, I asked him about it. What did it all mean? He paused, looked into my eyes, and said, "Are you ready to take this to the next level, to spend the rest of our lives together?" My answer, yes, came peacefully, knowing it was the next step for us. He asked me when I wanted to marry. I suggested October, in the coolness of early fall, to allow time to plan a wedding with both of our families present. He responded gingerly, "I think you'll make a beautiful June bride." Nine weeks, I said, was not enough time, but he assured me it could be done, so we settled on June 19 as our wedding day. It also happened to be my dad's birthday and Juneteenth Day, which is highly celebrated in the South. Later, I asked him about his unconventional wedding proposal, which was not what I had dreamed of, and laughed when he simply responded, "Sweetheart, this isn't Hollywood."

Moment of Reflection

Love doesn't follow a script.

 CHAPTER 10

The Wedding

And I will restore to you the years that the locust hath eaten, the cankerworm, and the caterpillar, and the palmerworm, my great army which I sent among you. And ye shall eat in plenty, and be satisfied, and praise the name of the Lord your God, that hath dealt wondrously with you: and my people shall never be ashamed.

—Joel 2:25–26 KJV

Our families were not surprised when we called them to announce our engagement. After nine months of courtship, we decided to have an outdoor wedding in the country, where Lee had experienced loss and would experience love again. My brother, Joe, agreed to give my hand to Lee in marriage. He respected Lee and thought he was a great match for his baby sister. I watched the two of them bond, only to wish that my father could be there. Dad had known my struggles and in his later years, wanted me to have someone special to love. Two days before his death, he spoke these last words of advice, which resonated in my heart: "Don't settle for just anyone. You have too much to offer, and you deserve a good man, someone who can love and appreciate you." He would have loved Lee, the man I was going to marry, who, like Dad, had served his country and enjoyed family life, hunting, and the simple things of life. My sisters often commented that Lee had ways like Dad, which was comforting at times, and made us feel like Dad was with us.

My daughters were happy to see the glow on their mother's face, jokingly reminding me that southern men love good food and need attending to. When I returned home, I got busy with wedding plans while carrying out my daily routines in the city. Lee's children graciously offered to help with wedding plans, on the other end because they were happy that their dad had found love again, someone to share his life with. Intuitively, I knew that the wedding would be a sweet and bitter experience for them. They had lost their mother five years earlier, and now their dad was taking on a new wife. I understood their loss and respectfully paid attention to their feelings. I wanted us to become one family because what they needed and how they felt during this transition was very important.

Lee, my sister, Erma, and I arrived at the courthouse, which had been built in 1883. It had all the southern charm of hardwood floors and a carved wooden banister that led to the second floor, which carried a musty smell of aged wood in the humid climate. The furnishings were reminiscent of another era, with historical documents hanging on the walls next to pictures of city pioneers from the past. Atop a wooden counter, we took our oaths as the clerk released to us a vintage-style license to wed with "Rites of Matrimony" printed in Baskerville Old Face font. Lee and I signed the wedding document and were instructed to wait thirty-six hours before holding our ceremony to become husband and wife. Later, we met Pastor Ron for lunch at the local diner to plan the ceremony.

We returned to the homestead where family and friends joined us as excitement filled the air in preparation for the wedding.

We created an outdoor chapel to exchange wedding vows under the big post oak tree in Lee's front yard. Guests sat in rows next to the aisle that led to an arch interwoven with big yellow roses. A large tent for 150 guests stood erected in the backyard next to the Mimosa tree visited by colorful mammoth butterflies and red cardinals. The local restaurateur catered a menu of catfish, chicken, hush puppies, green beans, and potato salad, complemented with fresh watermelons from the neighbor's patch. Two wedding cakes were delivered by noon: a three-tiered white cake with fresh daisies on top for the bride and a chocolate cake with chocolate shavings on top for the groom.

Lee gathered his grandsons to remove bull nettle from the field, so guests could park without burrs sticking to their skin and clothing. I was disappointed when the neighbor respectfully moved the cows that I wanted as a backdrop to another grazing field; he didn't think it was a good idea to have cows mooing during the ceremony. Carolyn, another sister, had picked black-eyed Susan early that morning to makes wildflower arrangements for the reception tables. Shirley and Joan, my bridesmaids, were busy wrapping a bouquet of coral- and cream-colored roses in satin ribbons. They all were there to support me, and we could only imagine what our mothers would have thought of it all. Erma, who had accompanied me on the piano, the first time I met Lee, was now practicing the wedding march on the piano he had purchased for the home we would share when visiting in the country.

The post oak tree gracefully provided shade as guests arrived. I peered through the bathroom window and noticed a dear friend sitting with her husband. They had traveled 2,900 miles from Bermuda to witness this special occasion. I paused and tried to savor the moment but succeeded only in part. I was living in the moment, preparing to marry the man I would love for a lifetime.

Lee had returned from his daughter's house dressed in a black pinstripe suit, waiting patiently while I put on my wedding attire. The procession began with the groom and groomsmen standing at the altar next to Pastor Ron. Lee stood next to

Thomas, who was proud of the fact that he had introduced his dad to his new bride. Our granddaughters walked down the aisle in tandem, dressed in delicate white frocks, sprinkling rose petals from a basket as the maid of honor and bridesmaids trailed behind them.

Lee's eyes latched onto mine with a smile of approval as I stepped out onto the front porch. I was wearing a beaded ecru lace gown with silk rosebuds in my hair and holding the bouquet of roses made especially for me by my maid of honor. As I stepped onto the porch, Joe gracefully escorted me to the altar, where he lovingly kissed me on the cheek and handed me to his future brother-in-law. Tears began to flow down Erma's face as she looked on and said, "You look so beautiful and happy." I could hear the birds singing above me in the post oak tree as we began to say our vows.

Pastor Ron had consulted with us before the wedding about our wishes for the ceremony. We had simply asked him to follow God's guidance. In doing so, he blessed our sacrament of communion, taken from a vintage, rose-colored goblet that he and his wife shared with us, to symbolize the unity of our covenant. As Lee raised the goblet to my lips, I thought about the quality of his character when he said, "You drink first." Our hearts surrendered to each other as we exchanged these words:

"Intreat me not to leave thee, or to return from following after thee: for whither thou goest, I will go; and where thou lodgest, I will lodge: thy people shall be my people, and thy God my God: Where thou diest, will I die, and there will I be buried: the Lord do so to me, and more also, if ought but death part thee and me" (Ruth 1:16–17 KJV).

Afterward, Pastor Ron announced, "You may kiss your bride," which Lee did with passion and love. We stood under the wedding bells of the arch as Pastor Ron introduced us as Mr. and Mrs. Johnson, followed by family and friends congratulating us with joy, tears, and all. The celebration continued with guests joining us for the reception, enjoying the bounty of food prepared for the occasion. Ironically, our appetites were of a different kind while we grazed on the food on our plates. Several guests made a toast to our happiness while my friend from Bermuda belted out a love ballad. The DJ began to play another love song that we had selected for our first dance, and Lee courageously took my hand and said,

"May I have this dance, Mrs. Johnson?" Everyone watched as he lovingly embraced me in his arms. I melted into his body with total satisfaction as we swayed to the melody, witnessing the blessing of God's hand as promised:

> I asked God for love to last a lifetime.
> In His infinite wisdom, He understood,
> Choosing the right season, time, and place
> To will His purpose, to honor my place.
> No one could have forecast His plan
> Or understood the blessings of His hands.
> In His infinite knowledge, He understood,
> Willing His best for two hearts that He loved.
> Unbridled devotion, He delivered with grace,
> Rooted deeply into what was once void space.
> Cultivating love with purpose to stand,
> Fulfilling our destiny, His promise, His plan.
> In His infinite knowledge, He understood
> The purpose of two hearts to love and to serve.
> No one could have forecast His plan
> Or anticipated the blessings of His hands.

Loved as Promised

EPILOGUE

I'm blessed to have experienced love as promised by the hand of God. It amazes me how He willed His purpose for my life. The Bible says that God is love, but I didn't understand the depth and scope of His love for many seasons. My perspective on love, seen through the eyes of the world, affected my self-worth, and I blamed myself for not being woman enough to sustain a relationship with a man. What I discovered, over time, was that no woman is enough to sustain a relationship with a man based solely on her physical attributes and intelligence. There is a spiritual aspect of our lives we must embrace. We are God's creation, and there is more to us than what we see. It's very important that we see ourselves as God sees us.

God reminds us, in Matthew 7:6 (KJV), "Give not that which is holy unto the dogs, neither cast ye your pearls before swine, lest they trample them under their feet, and turn again and rend you." Like many, I had casted my pearls into the wilderness of love and in return, reaped sorrow and disappointment. God's love for me would not let me self-destruct as I attempted to will my own way. God had a purpose beyond what I could forecast, and I had to trust and surrender to His plan for my life. I pondered this verse many times and sought to understand the significance of the pearl.

I decided to visit a pearl store and study the harvesting of pearls from around the world and this is what I learned. "The birth of a pearl begins when a foreign object lodges itself in the oyster's soft inner body. Unable to expel the intruder, the oyster protects itself by secreting and encasing the foreign object in a smooth, silky, hard crystalline substance known as "nacre." Layers and layers of nacre creates a smooth coating, which gives the pearl its beautiful shimmering iridescence, lustre, and a soft inner glow unlike any other gem. Pearls come in various shape, sizes, and colors, and continue to grow as long as they are embedded in the oyster. With the right amount of temperature, hibernating time, and nutrition, pearls are formed that are harvested as a miraculous creation of beauty." (http://www.americanpearl.com/ahistory.html.)

Like pearls, you are God's miraculous creation of beauty. Your pearls are all the qualities and talents that He has embedded inside of you to be cherished and valued. God invested time and special care to make you the person you are, not to be squandered or devalued but appreciated and loved. Please know that God has your best interests at heart and wants you to have what you deserve: the best. To have what God wants you to have, again I say that you must see yourselves as God sees you. Trust Him, for God is love.

The world seeks to understand what real love is. What better source is there than the one who possesses it, our heavenly Father? Jesus loves us so much that He declared His love in the book of John. "If ye abide in me, and my words abide in you, ye shall ask what ye will, and it shall be done unto you" (John 15:7 KJV). "As the Father hath loved me, so have I loved you: continue ye in my love" (John 15:9 KJV). "You did not choose Me, but I chose you and appointed you that you should go and bear fruit, and that your fruit should remain, that whatever you ask the Father in My name He may give you" (John 15:16 NKJV). God wants you to prosper, not just in love and marriage, but in all areas of your life with the pearls that He has given you. But first, you must embrace a personal relationship with Him. "For God so loved the world, that he gave his only begotten Son, that whosoever believeth in him should not perish, but have everlasting life" (John 3:16 KJV).

If you have not embraced God as your first love with heartfelt sincerity, this is where you can begin, by saying, "Heavenly Father, I have sinned and ask for your forgiveness. I confess that Jesus Christ is Lord, and that He died for my sins that I might be saved. I accept Jesus Christ as my Lord and Savior. Please come into my heart. Amen."

God's love is the glue that creates a special bond between a man and a woman for life. All the ways we desire to be loved and valued in a relationship come from our Creator: the ability to love unconditionally as He loves us unconditionally, to be faithful in our commitment as God is faithful to us, to freely serve each other with honor and respect. What greater honor is there than God sacrificing His most prized possession on our behalf, His son? Most importantly, we must have the ability to live with and forgive one another as God forgave us of our shortcomings and extended His grace. When you possess God as your first love, God will send you one of His chosen ones to love for a lifetime in His time.

God answered my prayer and granted me the love I desired. My husband and I vowed to embrace opportunities every day to appreciate the gift of love that God has given us. We enjoy God's blessing in the simple things of life, which are of great significance to us. Like our garden, our love continues to grow as we enjoy the bounty of God's blessing with intensity, devotion, and commitment. I encourage you to spend time getting to know your first love, and remember, don't settle for less; settle for more! Love can happen, and please know that God has not forgotten about you.

www.ingramcontent.com/pod-product-compliance
Lightning Source LLC
Chambersburg PA
CBHW021015090426
42738CB00007B/799